I0441209

Body Language Secrets For Men

Adjust Your Body Language To Your Advantage And Achieve Great Results In Life

Table of Contents

Introduction

I want to thank you and congratulate you for purchasing the book *Body Language Secrets for Men: Adjust Your Body Language To Your Advantage And Achieve Great Results In Life.*

This book contains proven steps and strategies on how to interpret body language and express the right signals to manipulate interactions to your advantage.

There are things in our lives we cannot control, but there are also those that we can. Many events and situations are beyond us, and you probably think that human interactions (how others approach, react, and speak to you) are among these.

Thanks to continuing studies, both scientists and psychologists have found a way to read and interpret body language. With the proper knowledge on the subject, not only will you be able to translate these actions to understand other people's feelings and intentions and read beyond their spoken words, you will also be able to control your own and harbor the response you want.

You may think this is a scientific subject, but never underestimate the power of body language. Understanding and emitting the right non-verbal signals is beneficial in many aspects of life. This can be your ticket to a good career standing (and of course, a possible promotion), successful flirting and dating, or your key to unlocking lies and deception.

Read on to discover the secrets to understanding body language.

Chapter 1: The Basics of Body Language

Everybody is familiar with the quote "first impressions last," but not everyone is aware of how it develops – and how it can be controlled or altered. Though there is no accurate measure, numerous studies suggest that body language can influence up to 90% in creating impressions. Before anyone speaks a word, perception towards another person is molded by consciously and unconsciously observing and interpreting body signals – and this is a two-way communication. A person receives kinetic signals and sends them at the same time.

For example, there are situations when one can easily conclude another person is annoyed even without verbally expression or feel the disappointment of a boss by the way he looks. In turn, the observer responds or communicates his feelings (and sometimes even thoughts) unknowingly. One might feel guarded against the annoyed person or anxious in the face of the disappointed boss. It is important to note that these signals are being observed by the other person as well.

The process of reading body language is oftentimes so automatic that it becomes more of a reflex. By learning how to scrutinize each aspect of the body and their corresponding signals, a person can immediately and accurately read another and adjust his body language to take control of the situation or gain favorable results.

Background, History and Evolution

Official scientific studies focused on body language began only recently. Debates as to whether it is inherited genetically (nature) or influenced environmentally (nurture) continues. However, it has been accepted to some degree that body language can be both.

According to Charles Darwin's evolutionary theory, facial expressions are consistent among all humans despite cultural differences. This theory was later tested by Paul Ekman, and the results proved that Darwin was right. The six universally recognized facial expressions are happiness, sadness, fear, disgust, surprise and anger. Less fundamental physical gestures like winking and hand movements along with personal space distances are generally accepted to depend on cultural and social influences.

Conversely, the process of reading body language is hard-wired into our brain – although it usually happens unconsciously. Oftentimes, this ability is what saves an individual from imminent threat. Almost everyone has had a close encounter with trouble once or twice in their lives – either against animals or other humans – and if not for the signals of the intention to attack, the person could not have processed an early escape.

The same goes for flirting, dating, and eventually, mating. There are situations where verbal communication is not enough to fully express feelings and reactions, for they can be subject to misinterpretation – considering as well that women translate words differently from men. In these cases, using body language is the best option to communicate feelings.

Throughout history, body language has been used and interpreted, not only to avoid personal conflicts or reinforce attraction, but also to determine war. During the time when discovering new lands was prevalent and language between two completely different cultures had not been established, tribal leaders would rely on body language to decide whether to trust the foreigners, raise defense, or initiate an attack.

A more extensive scrutiny of non-verbal signals that still resonates with modern times happened during the time of the American Wild West – in games of poker. Players are keen on reading non-verbal signals and careful in displaying their own.

On a different note, reading non-verbal communication is very common in fields where people work with animals, like shepherds and animal trainers. This is the only way for animals to communicate with people, so humans had to learn to interpret animal body language, and vice versa, to herd and teach simple commands.

Prior to all of this, our cavemen ancestors relied solely on body language to communicate during the time before language was established. Due to evolutionary adaptation, women developed a keener perception and interpretation of non-verbal signals to reduce their physical vulnerability against males. This survival instinct had been carried until today, giving females an advantage in this area.

Prerequisites of Body Language Analysis

Learning the scope of non-verbal signs is necessary to accurately interpret body language. Other sources may give different definitions and may be limited to body positions and gestures. In this book, however, anything communicated non-verbally will be covered and discussed. The following list details the different aspects of body language:

- Body position
- Proxemics – or the space between two persons and how it changes
- Facial expression
- Eyes – their movement and focus (a person can maintain a blank facial expression, but how his eyes move often holds more meaning, making it important to separate this from the previous aspect)
- Touch (hand movements) – how one touches himself (scratch on the nose, wipe in the eye, brush through the hair, etc.) and how one connects with inanimate objects (pen, glasses, clothing, cigarettes, etc.)

When reading or interpreting a person's body signals, one must take all of these into consideration. Non-verbal communication analysis relies on several factors. Conclusions may immediately arise upon reading a single gesture, but this often leads to misinterpretations.

One must also know the aspects that could influence and alter the meaning of these signals. Below are some factors that should be analyzed before making any judgments.

1. Context

A signal may hold a different meaning depending on the situation. One must first examine and consider preceding events as well as the environment.

For example, a person crossing his arms may not be indicative of being defensive but instead merely keeping warm. In other cases, nose scratching may not mean the concealment of a lie but simply that the person's nose is itchy.

2. Evidence

As explained earlier, a single signal may lead to misinterpretation, so looking for supporting signs is necessary for accurate conclusions. Much like in other disciplines, especially in crime investigations, one must have more than one piece of evidence to support a claim because there can be cases when a signal may mean two or more different things.

3. Culture and Ethnicity

Although general facial expressions are recognized across the world, there are gestures and signals that vary from culture to culture. This is especially important to take note of in this generation because societies are becoming more ethnically diverse. One good example is how comfortable personal space distances differ from Westerners to Easterners. Should there be a female Asian employee in a North American company, the supervisor may be accused of sexual harassment for innocently putting his hand on her shoulder.

4. Age and Gender

Consider the type of person and the situation in assessing body language, especially in terms of measuring the strength of the signal and its meaning. A gesture may mean less to one person but holds more to another in a different event. Young men are often energetic and may display many pronounced gestures. While, in contrast, older women have less energy and maintain modest postures, preventing exhibitions of pronounced body signals.

5. Deception

Some people intentionally alter their outward body language to create a specific impression, and it can range from direct eye contact to a firm handshake. This is common for politicians and salespeople. In conjunction to the second factor, one must be able to see beyond isolated signals and seek more evidence to prevent superficial analysis.

Reading subtle gestures (like the twitching of the corner of the mouth, the contracting of pupils, or lifting of an eyebrow) can uncover hidden motives and true meanings. These "micro gestures" are subconscious and difficult to spot. Plus, they cannot be controlled, thus in the abovementioned situations, they prove to be useful. Lie spotting will be explained in Chapter 4.

6. Signs of Weakness

People may sometimes exhibit negative signals (boredom, insecurity, disinterest, anxiety, etc.), and the person interpreting them may immediately conclude these as signs of weakness. Before making any assumptions, it is important to note of any external factors affecting the individual under observation, for it is often the situation, not the person, that produces these despite the strength and confidence one carries. The following are some circumstances that may induce negative feelings or signs:

- Presence of authority or dominant figure (boss or teacher)
- Information overload
- Fatigue
- Stress
- Unfavorable weather conditions
- Hunger or thirst
- Health disorders or complications
- Intoxicants
- Unfamiliarity or change
- Being part of the minority

All of these factors can affect an individual's body language and therefore, must be considered before drawing any conclusions.

Take special note of the prerequisites of body language analysis because your level of understanding in this will determine your effectiveness in interpreting nonverbal signals. The following chapters will construct settings and describe in detail signs that will be commonly encountered in the corresponding situations. Keep in mind, however, that nothing is absolute, and the interpretations suggested may have different meanings when you apply or encounter them personally, thus the need to fully grasp the prerequisites.

Chapter 2: Body Language in Business and Office

In the past, men were hunters by profession and the jungle was their office. They were adept at reading animal behavior and especially sharp when brought face-to-face with a predator. These hunters knew when to attack, raise defense, or back-off – all relying on nonverbal signals. They even knew which animals to befriend and train.

Although man has evolved, the same can be said of our modern working environment. The office is our new jungle, and we need to identify threats from friends for the sole purpose of survival – hence, the need to bring out the inner hunter.

Reading Signs and Signals

Reading people inside the office can be beneficial in many ways. Body language can unravel motives, pinpoint team players, and reveal superiors' hidden thoughts. Knowing these can give a person an advantage by being aware of how to behave in the working environment and having an idea who to give trust to. For bosses, this will give them a notion of which employees are good followers and which only pretend to be.

Below are a few signs that can help in determining the above said aspects.

1. Eyes

> Direct eye contact is the most basic giveaway in body language but also the easiest to control. Dishonesty or shame in one's words can be read when a person tends to avoid eye

contact during conversations. In contrast, those who maintain it show interest in the topic. However, remember to search for supporting evidence before making conclusions. A person may keep his eyes on the receiver out of politeness, or because he too has knowledge in body language.

2. Hands

Colleges and universities often teach graduating students to give a firm handshake during job interviews to exhibit confidence. This much is true, but the hands can reveal more from a person. Anxiety oftentimes triggers rapid tapping. Hands are also a way to subconsciously demonstrate dominance. When a person rubs or taps them together, they are displaying supremacy. On the other hand, when they are placed together to form a steeple, it generally states *"I am in charge, and I want you to know that"*. It can also be used to give comfort and reassurance when one is casually placed on top of the other.

3. Posture

Dominance or confidence is often demonstrated by puffing the chest out and keeping a tall shoulder. Slouching during a conversation may mean the person is questioning the statements of the other.

4. Standing

A person who holds his hands behind his back usually commands attention, but this can also be an expression of frustration or anger. As for those who plant their hands on their hips, they are often full of aggression.

5. Stroking

The act of stroking one's cheeks or chin is usually a "do not disturb" sign, for the person could be deep in thought. A supervisor may look he's not doing anything and free to talk, but if he's doing this gesture, it's best to postpone whatever requires his attention as long as it's not urgent.

6. Yawning

Outside the office, this can simply mean the person is tired. However, in the working environment, this is typically a demonstration of boredom with the task at hand or with the conversation.

7. Aversion of Eyes

There are times in the middle of a conversation when the other person would rub his eye and look away briefly. This is often dismissed, but it is actually a display of disbelief.

8. Touching the Nose

This is usually regarded as a negative reaction, for constantly rubbing and touching of the nose indicates doubt, rejection or that the person is lying.

9. Crossed Arms

Many may interpret this as a show of anger but it is, in fact, a demonstration of defense. This gesture is best recognized and not provoked. The right way to handle the situation would be to initiate a calmer discussion over tea or coffee.

10. Fidgeting

When a person finds it difficult to sit still during meetings, it means he might have more important things to do. Outside this setting, however, it could mean that he is anxious or has something on his mind.

11. Playing with Hair

People who constantly hold or curl their hair generally have low-esteem and feel shy around others. It is basically a display of insecurity and doubt.

Take note that these are body signals commonly exhibited inside the office. There can be a variety of other gestures that can support a conclusion. Remember, however, to look for clusters of evidence before confirming interpretations. As described earlier, outside factors can also affect a person's body language.

Nonetheless, the basic signs above are a quick guide to understanding people inside the office.

Understanding these can help an individual tune in to his co-workers or even avoid difficult situations.

Applying Body Language

Reading people is one thing, controlling one's body language is quite another. When dealing with people, especially potential clients and higher-ups, or when heading groups and presentations, maintaining the proper body posture can help produce favorable results.

The following are common business- or work-related situations and the best body language for each.

Meeting a Potential Client

Establishing trust is the primary goal in this situation. The client must feel comfortable and a working relationship should already be developed in this first meeting. Aside from keeping direct eye-contact and exuding confidence, the following tips will further help in reaching these goals:

Tips:

- *Mirroring* is the best and fastest way to establish rapport. This is the act of mimicking the other person's posture, tone and attitude. This will make an individual appear non-threatening, and it makes the other comfortable.

- *Keeping a reasonable distance* is another key in supporting positive body language. Staying close, but not uncomfortably so, shows respect for the client's personal space while keeping interest in what he has to say. The guide in maintaining distance is as follows:

- Intimate: 17 inches and below
- Personal: 18 inches to 4 feet
- Social: 4 feet to 8 feet
- Public: 8 feet and beyond

- *Never move back* when the client is speaking. It will create the feeling of being disrespected when the receiver backs away.

Presentation of Pitch

The goal of presentations is to maintain the audience's attention and interest and to communicate the contents using physical gestures to emphasize points and important details. Maintaining the proper tone, volume, pace and pauses are necessary, but non-verbal signals determine the strength of the delivery. Below are important body language tips for successful presentations:

Tips:

- *Refrain from looking at the computer or screen.* A presenter should know the contents by heart. A quick glance is alright, but powerful presentations are made by those who keep their eyes on the audience.
- *Keep eye contact with the audience.* In conjunction with the first tip, a presenter may refrain from looking at his

presentation and know the content per slide, but keeping his eyes on the wall across the room will not send the message through. He has to hold the attention of his coworkers and keep his presentation interesting.

- *Lean toward the audience when emphasizing important points.* According to studies, effective communication relies on 55% body language, 38% tone of voice and 7% words. With this in mind, a person remembers and understands a message when it is said with complementing body signals.

Leading a Team

Establishing dominance without being aggressive can be achieved by properly positioning the body. This is necessary to gain the confidence and trust of team members and maintain unquestionable leadership. Of course, performance and decision-making skills play a big part in this, but in setting the right impression, the following tips will be beneficial:

Tips:

- *Head should be kept high.* This communicates supremacy. Although be careful on how high the head is held because this can also convey arrogance.
- *Keep the shoulders back and the spine straight.* Exuding confidence will give team members a reason to grant the leader their trust.
- *Lean forward when talking.* Leaning forward is necessary to lessen the air of

arrogance exhibited when the head is held high. Plus, the speaker will hold the attention of the targeted listeners.

- *Lean back to encourage others to talk.* Verbally expressing the intention may lead to a different, and sometimes negative, interpretation. Letting the body speak is the safest way to express encouragement.

There are other diverse events in the office that require the power of body language, but the three situations stated above are the most common and sensitive in the working environment and in business.

Nonverbal communication in this setting is not limited to the above enumerated gestures. There are more signs and signals that can help decipher a person's thoughts and feelings, and they will be discussed further in chapter 5.

Chapter 3: Body Language in Dating

Reading body language in flirting and dating proves to be immensely beneficial for men. Males tend to be more straightforward and to the point. Whatever they say, they mean it. However, the same cannot be expected from their female counterparts, making it difficult for men to decode them. Women tend to be more complex – like a puzzle. What they say might not be exactly what they mean.

In these cases, the best way to unlock their thoughts, feelings and desires is by reading their non-verbal signals. Ladies can alter their words, but their body speaks it all; it just needs to be decoded. Display of sexual availability between men and women is extremely different. Female signals are subtle, discreet and often directed to one person only.

On the other hand, male flirting is like a bat signal – everyone in the room knows he's available. It's not solely because women are more skilled with body language. There is a deeper scientific explanation for this. Even among other species of animals, it's the females who lead the chase, and men only respond to their availability and permissions. This is a mating behavior that has evolved over thousands of years and remains an instinct to each and every one today.

Fertility bestows the most influence in this courtship ritual. Women are sexually active when they are fertile, and as every reproductive teacher notes, this happens only once a month. Men, however, produce sperm everyday making them available and active almost anytime.

Expressing Availability

In this world's modern setting, hunting for a mate initially begins in a bar. This is a common place where young and available people hang out and display their sexuality. It will be crowded, and not to mention, competition will be in every corner of the room. Each and every man will do their best to attract females. Keep in mind, however, that it is the opposite sex who selects and leads, so the best way to stay ahead of the game is to stand out – exuding the right body language will do the trick.

- Posture. The most basic way to stand out is to have the right posture. Just like a soldier, keep the back straight, pull the shoulders back, push the chest out, and suck in the stomach. Maintain an erect posture and act like the tallest man in the room. This will give an air of confidence and supremacy over other males.

- Legs. Always keep them apart to increase size. This is an illusion of course, but looking bigger than the rest will give the idea that this specific man is the alpha, and women's instincts are to target the most dominant male for mating.
- Hands and Arms. One eye-catching position of the hands is when they are pointing to the genital area. This can be as subtle as putting both hands in your jeans pocket with the thumbs jutting out and pointing to the crotch area, or by doing the cowboy stance where the thumbs are hanging on the belt loops with the fingers, again, aimed at the direction of the genitals. This is also an effective way to

increase size by spreading the arms out. According to studies, the top two male body parts the ladies' eyes are drawn to are the biceps and the crotch area, so maximize these aspects by positioning your arms and hands correctly.

- <u>Eyes</u>. Staring does not work for males the same way it does for females. In most cases, this veers more toward the creepy side than a seductive one. Never fix the eyes on one place. Move them along with the head to scan the room from time to time. Females will read this gesture and yes, this translates to, *"I am available."* This also makes a good technique for catching who is checking you out.

These well-pronounced body language tools will surely be noticed by the ladies in the bar. Next, keep an eye out for women showing interest and giving out signals for you to come over and flirt.

Women's Display of Attraction

It's often difficult to know whether a woman is interested in a man or not. Most of the time, males miss and fail to interpret the signals females give out. Making the first move is not a popular option for the ladies, but when they see a guy they like from across the room, they will exhibit different non-verbal signs that roughly translate as a green-light for the man to initiate flirting and intimacy. Below is some of the body language that indicates their interest:

- <u>Eyes</u>. This is the very first body part that should be looked at for evidence. Women may constantly look at the man they like, and they intentionally let the guys catch them staring. Expert flirts would even put extra seduction in their eyes that obviously speaks "come-hither".

- <u>Hands</u>. Observe where her hands touch. A lady may fiddle with her accessories, adjusting bracelets or tugging necklaces, and this means she's nervous and excited at the same time. These gestures are often an outlet for the positive tension she feels. Some signs are excused like when a woman touches herself in the neck, hair, cleavage, thigh, etc. These are actually subconscious imaging of how their person of desire would touch them that way.

- <u>Hair</u>. Bouncy and animated locks are the best flirting weapon of females. Playing with the hair, tucking it behind her ears, or flipping it is a display of interest and attraction. Plus, it draws attention.

- <u>Foot and Knees</u>. The direction where or to whom it points to is often the person of interest.

- <u>Lips</u>. Attracted women constantly smile and laugh more often regardless of whether a conversation is funny or not. Another significant hint of interest is when she licks her lips. Psychologists say this mimics the female labia, hence the red lipstick (which suggests increased blood flow), and the constant moistening. Pouting can also indicate attraction. Although, do not mistake this for the pout with the protruding lower lip for this means she's upset. A sexual pout is one that looks like the initial forming of a kiss.

- Head. When she tilts her head, she exposes her neck, a soft vulnerable area and also an erogenous zone. The same effect is created when she exposes her inner wrists and forearms.

- Posture. A woman will naturally straighten her posture to answer to the urge of looking more appealing. Just like how men do it, she will push her chest out, suck her stomach in, and stand or sit taller.

Note that a man requires a combination of these evidences to fully conclude that a lady is actually flirting. Relying on the expression of only one signal does not fully justify female attraction.

Proper Response of Men

In the event females display these gestures, males should know how to play along. Some may notice the attraction building and immediately confront the lady about it by straightforwardly and verbally reciprocating their interest. Women may respond negatively to that. As explained in the first chapter, they are more adept to body language than men due to an evolutionary adaptation. Hence, the perfect response for her flirtatious gestures is by talking in the same language.

How to respond when she makes eye contact:

- <u>Eyes</u>. Acknowledge the gesture by holding the contact. She will avert or lower her gaze, but don't take this as disinterest. This is typical for women. As explained earlier, she will constantly look at the direction of their person of desire. Slightly raising the eyebrows is a more pronounced way to recognize her eye contact, and to express your intention to flirt back.

- <u>Mouth</u>. Smiling is the best way to confirm if she's flirting or just constantly looking at you because of that spaghetti stain on your shirt. For added seduction and to express flirtation, opt for a cheeky smile. If she smiles back, congratulations.

- <u>Preening</u>. Adjusting a tie, straightening the shirt, or running hands over hair gives her the idea that the man is ready to play and have a good time. As early as this stage, she could begin mirroring you. If she does the same, especially when she brushes her hair and exposes her underarm, it's time to reduce the distance between you and her.

Flowing through upon direct contact:

Typically, it's the man who walks over to the lady. Though, keep in mind that if she's the aggressive kind, she might initiate the first move. Whoever decides to, it's best to keep the following body language in mind when talking and flirting.

The body language of women enumerated earlier are exhibited and strengthened during this stage.

- <u>Space</u>. Reduce the distance but remember to not get too close. Refer to the guide in maintaining distance explained in the previous chapter. Standing or sitting opposite another person by rule of thumb is confrontational. However, in flirting, this helps in maintaining eye-contact, and it optimizes engagement. Leaning forward is a good and non-creepy way to express interest and attraction. Plus, it's a good way to measure how intimate she's willing to get.

- <u>Arms</u>. Avoid crossing your arms because it signals disinterest, so it is best to keep them open.

- <u>Touch</u>. Another good way to know if she is highly interested is if the male accidentally (from the man's perspective, however, this is intentional) touches her, like lightly brushing against her arms or hands. If she backs away, it could mean she hasn't made up her mind quite yet. Don't be discouraged, though. This could only mean she's not ready to reduce the physical space and move on to intimate flirting. Further reinforcement of comfort and rapport will eventually lead to it.

  Before initiating with this body language, however, let her do it first. Typically, it's the females who make excuses to touch the man's hands, arms or legs -- she could be picking a fallen hair on your shoulder, or stretching her legs to "unintentionally" bump yours. The important thing when she does this is to be a gentleman and reciprocate.

- <u>Mirroring</u>. Much like in body language for business, building rapport relies in synchronizing gestures with the opposite sex. Much like in the concept of touch explained previously, returning the favor is a healthy expression of interest and attraction. She may initiate other gestures like leaning forward. When she does so, you can do the same.

Keep in mind, however, that verbal communication is equally important in flirting and dating. These body language tips are just a way for you to read past the spoken words of women.

Dating and flirting may happen in many varied situations, and the above stated setting may not always apply. Expression of attraction does not exclusively happen in a bar, for example. Women may exude interest while dining with friends in a restaurant, or when quietly sitting in the train on the way home. What's important is to be quick in recognizing and acknowledging these signals -- especially the discrete ones – because failing to do so will infer lack of interest, and they are unlikely to repeat the signs.

Chapter 4: Spotting Deception

It's not only inside the office that the need to spot deception arises. For managers and employers, this skill is quite beneficial. However, our modern economy is filled with threats, often caused and brought upon by fellow human beings. Reading through lies, dishonesty and deception can actually save us from trouble and wasting hard-earned money.

With the onset of different products and services (such as real estate, beauty and health products, insurance, etc.) that are available for sale, we sometimes find ourselves falling into a scam without knowing it. Salespeople will blast self-confidence so effectively and wear the best suits so fashionably that an innocent person would immediately invest trust in everything they say, only to find out later that they are scammers.

Another scenario where lie spotting can play a role is with friends and even with a significant other. Friends come and go, especially for a person with a very active social life. Some will enter and even force their way to your life with a motive. Though it may not be a bad intention, it's best to know if there are any to avoid surprises or to be able to defend oneself from the possibility of trouble. As for a significant other, knowing if she's hiding secrets can be helpful. She could be planning to move out or break-up, or worse, she could be cheating.

For whatever purpose it may serve, learning how to spot lies can be a necessity.

What to look for in Facial Expressions

Remarkably, the human face is capable of exhibiting 10,000 different expressions out of its 43 muscles. Thankfully, knowing all of them is not necessary to spot deception. The best thing about the face is that not all of its expressions can be controlled and it often reveals a person's genuine feelings or thoughts – making it easier to spot lies. Below are some general guidelines when reading a person's face to uncover dishonesty.

1. The Power of Symmetry

As discussed in the first chapter, facial expressions can be grouped to six general emotions, namely happiness, fear, surprise, anger, sadness and disgust. Thanks to the extensive study by Paul Ekman, he proved that our faces express these symmetrically. When the face muscles move in accordance to these emotions, both sides exhibit or reveal the corresponding feeling. Therefore, asymmetrical facial expressions indicate a lie. For example, if a surprise for a colleague at work is revealed and only one side of his face shows the signs of shock, chances are he already knew about it.

2. Spotting Micro-Expressions

This, by far, is the most difficult skill to develop. The reason why these expressions are tagged as "micro" is because they flash very briefly across the face – 1/25th of a second to be precise. Genuine emotions always instantly appear, and it takes a split-second before a person can consciously or subconsciously neutralize them. These are the best giveaways to know if an individual is lying or hiding something. However, detecting these will take practice and extensive knowledge in body language, especially facial expressions.

3. Smiles and Eyes

Genuine smiles involve both the upper and lower portions of the face. Of course, the mouth plays a big part in this. However, deciphering whether it's true or fake depends on the upper. There is such a term as "smiling eyes" because an honest smile has them. When the eyes narrow and lines (or "crow's feet" as some may call it) appear at the sides, it's a true smile. The best way to practice scrutinizing one from the other is by looking at selfies and candid photos (those that feature a laughing or smiling person).

Try covering the bottom half of the face in these pictures, and focus on the expression of the upper half. If happiness can be felt or seen in the eyes, it's genuine. On the other hand, if it seems neutral, then the smile is not genuine. Therefore, if a lover's smile didn't touch the top half of her face (or if only one side exhibited the emotion) upon asking if she's alright, she's probably not and she's hiding it from you.

4. Sadness is Reflected in the Chin

It is easy to angle the sides of the mouth downward when faking sadness. However, it is nearly impossible to keep the chin from moving. When a person exhibiting this emotion is insincere, there will always be extra chin movement.

5. Maintained Eye Contact

It is common belief that when a person cannot maintain eye contact, he is lying. However, even when stating completely honest words, a person still has the tendency to look away or down. In fact, it is when an individual maintains or stretches eye contact that one should be wary because liars believe that if they do this, their story would be believed in. Many are serving jail time because they have been wrongfully convicted by the jury for the simple reason they were not able to maintain eye contact. The direction the eyes look often bears varied meanings, and it does not always denote insincerity. These meanings will be further explained in the following chapter.

What to note in Body Language

It has been discussed in the earlier chapters of this book that body language contributes most to effective communication. However, many of us rely heavily on verbal expressions and word use to get the desired message and emotions across when, in fact, we should rely most on our body signals. The same goes with liars. They tend to practice their lines and control their tone when expressing a statement, but seldom do they master their gestures.

Inconsistencies are often the giveaway when observing both verbal and nonverbal signals. What the liar says might not match how he acts. The following are some body signals and signs that may denote insincerity.

1. Head

Fabricating a story takes up much of a person's attention and focus that there is a high probability that he would be unable to match the movements of his head with his words. A liar may say "no," but his head will reflexively nod when lying to a question.

2. Face

The stress of lying increases tension and the person will automatically and unconsciously relieve this by constantly touching his face. A liar may touch his neck, throat and mouth, or scratch his nose or behind the ear.

3. Shoulders

Much like in facial expressions, asymmetry in shoulder gestures denotes deception. We can express varied emotions and thoughts through this underrated body part, such as exasperation when it drops, discomfort when it hunches up, or "I don't know" or "I don't care" when it shrugs. Genuine gestures are complete and symmetrical. Both shoulders either rise or fall when expressing honest feelings. If a person, however, moves just one side when answering a question, he is being dishonest or pretending.

4. Torso

The body tends to be more animated when telling a story. A person leans forward when emphasizing a point, and leans back when concluding a part. When someone narrating an account, on the other hand, looks and feels awkward, and hand gestures are limited and confined within a certain space, take precaution. Stiffness can denote fabrication because liars tend to freeze to avoid exposing too much emotive body language. Another clue would be when the body is not facing the accuser directly, because of the discomfort the guilty one feels.

5. Arms

In conjunction to the previous number, the underuse of hands during a conversation is a big clue in spotting lies, especially if the person crosses them. This is a defensive posture, and the individual may be keeping himself locked because of the thought he might leak clues to his deception. Open arms with the palms out is the opposite of this gesture and this denotes truthfulness and honesty.

6. Hands

Much like the arms, when the person keeps their hands in one place or limits their actions, he could be stating deceitful words. People narrating a genuine story tend to use their hands to embellish their account; if a person doesn't, there's a huge chance he himself is not invested in his statements. Other clues would be closed first or folded palms (this indicates restraint), or when the liar exaggerates the size or placement of something with his gestures.

7. Legs

This body part can reveal much information about a person's state of mind because these are harder to consciously control. When someone unusually broadens his stance, this could mean he is asserting dominance – a defensive mechanism when a person feels weak. Another sign is when the person rubs his thighs. This is an action that releases tension. In the presence of higher authority (this applies more appropriately in an office setting), an employee could splay his legs as a display of territory – another defensive posture.

8. Ankles

Locked ankles when seated or reclined is a display of anxiety. Despite looking and sounding calm, a person feels discomfort when he does this gesture. Standing during a conversation, on the other hand, with crossed ankles indicates high mental activity.

9. Feet

Where the feet points is usually the direction where the person want to go. If it's directed at the door, then he could be dying to leave the room. Another indication of nerves is when an individual taps his foot. This, however, may or may not imply deception or dishonesty. Gestures made by this body part should be considered with other signs to produce a viable conclusion.

10. Space

Setting-up physical barriers is a person's initial response when threatened, especially when he is hiding something. These can take the form of a bag, a book, or a coffee cup, and they are placed between the interrogator and the interviewee. Much like how a guilty person would sit in the farthest chair, this act is to increase his "safety zone." When suspecting deception, the best way to react to this gesture is by removing the objects.

Verbal and Nonverbal Contradictions

For this section of the book, discussions will be mixed with a brush-up of verbal inconsistencies. Focusing solely on body language in this chapter may result to false suspicions.

Lies aren't only shown in body language, but also in the manner of speaking. Disparity between these two is the best indicators of deception. A dishonest person is so focused on altering his words that he often leaves his gestures unattended, thus revealing his true feelings and intentions.

1. Emotions vs. Words vs. Gestures

True feelings are simultaneously expressed by words, facial expressions and gestures. For example, a surprised person would exhibit the emotion in her face, raise her hands to her mouth, and express the words "Oh my gosh!" all at the same time. However, if one of these is delayed, the person could be faking her emotion. When asking someone if his food is delicious for instance, and he replied "I love it!" but the smile came after instead of together, he is not completely invested in his statement.

2. Expression vs. Statements

If an ex-girlfriend of yours forced you to watch a recent trilogy about vampires, you'd know exactly what this contradiction means. Insincere words are accompanied by off facial expressions. For example, the leading lady of the said movie stated, "Why can't you see how perfectly happy I am?" but her face didn't show any trace of it – in fact, she looked stressed – she's not feeling happy at all. Another good case would be when a girl says a simple "I love you" while frowning, there's a huge chance she might not or she herself is questioning the statement.

3. Timing

The pace of emotions is erratic when a person is being dishonest. Emotions are either delayed, expressed longer than normal, suddenly stopped, or a combination of all three.

4. Limited

Much like how smiling with the eyes work, emotions are expressed by the whole face. Expressions of a liar, on the other hand, are limited to the mouth.

Keep in mind that observing a person exhibiting these signs may not always mean they are being deceptive. As discussed in the first chapter, a gesture can be influenced by a number of factors, and these have to be taken into consideration before making any conclusions.

Chapter 5: General Body Language Translations

The body signs and signals in the previous chapters are focused more on specific situations. The same gestures can be committed in a different event but may hold a different meaning. Knowing the varied translations of each act can provide a wider perspective and produce a more accurate conclusion when interpreting another person's thoughts or emotions.

Below is a comprehensive list of body parts, gestures and their corresponding interpretations.

Eyes

The underlined words refer to the position of the eyes.

Right (generally) - Guessing, storytelling, lying

A person is generally fabricating stories when he looks to his right. This, however, does not necessarily mean he is lying. It all depends on the context of your conversation. Most of the time, it merely denotes an individual is touching his creative side.

Left (generally) - Recalling, remembering

This mainly suggests that an individual is accessing his memories to retrieve remembered facts. Most of the time, this is associated with telling the truth, but again, it all depends on other factors.

Upper-Right - Visualizing

When the person is supposed to be recalling facts and he happens to look in this direction, he's fabricating or lying. Otherwise, this denotes access to the brain's creative side and imagination.

Sideways Right - Construction of sounds

Imagining what a person said or would say is displayed by this eye movement. Similar with the previous account, this involves imagination, but is more focused on sound.

Lower-Right - Evaluating feelings

It could mean that the person is questioning how he feels. This is also related to the creative side but does not necessarily imply fabrication.

Upper-Left - Recalling images

Same as with looking left generally. A good sign if a person is meant to state facts, for it means he is telling the truth.

Sideways Left - Recalling sounds

This is similar with sideways right in terms of auditory responses. The difference is that when a person looks left, he is recalling sounds (like what his friend said earlier that day) from memory.

Lower-Left - Rationalizing

If lower-right suggests access to feelings -- which is directed more towards a person, like the evaluation of oneself -- looking down-left signifies self-talk or the processing of an outward view.

Sustained Eye-contact (when speaking) - Honesty or faked honesty

As discussed in the previous chapter, direct eye-contact denotes truthfulness. However, liars tend to control their eyes and adapt to this body language to appear sincere.

Sustained Eye-contact (when listening) - Interest

This can either mean interest towards the topic or attraction to the speaker.

Mouth

Fake Smile

It was explained in the preceding chapter how to determine a real smile from a fake one. Typically, this is a display of restrained displeasure, or the person is probably forced to agree.

Silent Smile - Secrecy

The teeth do not show and this basically is just a straight line across the face -- also called the tight-lipped smile. Smiling this way means the person is withholding his true feelings or thoughts, which can either be a secret he is not willing to share, distrust or rejection.

Twisted Smile

This can denote sarcasm, or a show of mixed-feelings -- depending on the context or statement of the individual. Under chapter 5, a lopsided expression can mean dishonesty or deception.

Protruding Bottom Lip - Upset

Jutting the lower lip is an impulse in crying. Adults may be able to hold the tears, but this gesture is a reflex when feeling upset. Although, people cry for a number of reasons, this expression may imply that the person is seeking sympathy or trying to thwart an attack.

Lip Biting - Tension

This can also mean high concentration. Otherwise, a person biting his lip is likely to be anxious.

Pursing Lips

Depending on the context of the situation or the conversation, this can mean a lot of things. Much like with the silent smile, a person may be pursing his lips to suppress a secret or withhold an emotion. Other interpretations of this could be impatience or anxiousness.

Head

Held Up - Alertness

Neutrality is basically the interpretation of this gesture. A person with his head held up is actually attentively listening without any bias.

Held High

This signal can be interpreted in different ways depending on the context. When a person is among subordinates, this is an expression of supremacy. In the face of threat, however, this can denote fearlessness. In normal settings, this shows arrogance.

Tilted to One Side - Thinking, non-threatening

A signal best read with other gestures for it can either mean submission or thoughtfulness. Tilting the head to the side will expose the neck -- a showcase of vulnerability – hence, expressing trust. In other situations, however, this can mean the person is sizing up the subject or topic by literally changing his perspective.

Tilted Downward - Criticism

People of authority are usually the ones who exhibit this gesture. When they do, they are expressing their disapproval or criticism.

Chin Up

The expression "chin up" literally means what it implies in body language. Pulling the chin up lifts the sternum, allowing the person to draw air in, puff the chest, and broaden the shoulders – exhibiting a stance of confidence. Much like holding the head high, a person keeping his chin up shows resilience, strength and pride.

Arms

Folded

Most of the time, this body signal represents protection by creating a barrier to the body. However, depending on the situation or context, this can mean many things. It can range from acrimony, boredom or tiredness from maintaining attention to something.

Folded with Clenched Fist

Clenched fists are the expression of hostility. Combined with folded arms, this may imply stubbornness, disdain or aggression.

Holding Own Upper Arms

This can be noted as self-hugging – a way to console oneself from unhappy or unsafe feelings. Generally, this act is connected to insecurity.

Held Behind the Body with Hands Clasped

This gesture is commonly used by those in power (politicians, the royal family, officers, policemen and even teachers). It expresses confidence and authority.

Other arm signals that hold meaning are generally those that serve as barriers to protect the body -- like when touching the shoulder using the opposite arm, or when an arm crosses the body to clasp the other. These indicate nervousness, along with other gestures where objects are involved like holding a bag, drink, or paper in front of the body. For males, the same can be denoted when they cover the genital area.

Hands

Open Palms

This gesture generally states openness. It was believed to have come from the act of showing the palms to demonstrate no weapons are held. Again, depending on the context, this can either mean submission, expression of honesty and trustworthiness, or seeking appeal.

Palms Down

When a person moves his lower arm across the body, palms down, it could mean he is expressing defiance, disagreement, authority or dominance.

Finger Pointing (at a person)

Generally, this is confrontational and dictatorial, and is often used by older people on young ones. However, when acted on other adults, this denotes arrogance and lack of social awareness or self-control.

Hand Chop

This gesture can either mean the discussion is over or the speaker is emphasizing a point.

Clenched Fist

Different meanings can be derived from this body signal, and is highly recommended to be interpreted along with other signals. It can arise from resistance, aggression, or determination, depending on the context or situation.

Knuckle-Cracking

Depending on who exhibits the gesture, it can either mean comforting oneself or seeking attention. It is usually denoted as an expression of male machismo.

Interwoven Fingers

When the hands are rested on a table, held across the stomach or on the lap, with the fingers interwoven, the person is either feeling frustrated, anxious or negative.

Thumbs Inside Closed Fist

Thumbs are flexible tools and locking them in the other fingers disables their readiness for action. This can mean the person is comforting himself, feeling insecure, or is simply frustrated.

Touching Nose (While speaking)

Telling lies and noses are well associated with each other because of Pinocchio's tale. It was said that a person naturally touches the nose when being dishonest to hide the redness caused by increased blood flow.

Pinching the Bridge of the Nose

This is a common gesture during meetings and presentations. When the boss displays this gesture, be afraid for it means you're going to get a negative evaluation.

Scratching the Neck

A gesture made when the person distrusts what was said. It was believed to have evolved from the need to protect the neck (a vulnerable area) when feeling doubt.

Hands through Hair

The person running a hand through his hair is either flirting or feeling exasperated. Looking for other evidences or analyzing contexts can support a proper conclusion.

Hands in Pocket

Inactive hands means the person is not ready for action or is not expressing interest in the situation. It can also be an exhibition of boredom or apathy.

Body signals are not limited to the above examples. There can be hundreds to thousands of non-verbal signs, but these are the ones we usually encounter and they hold much meaning. Looking for a combination is necessary to arrive at a sound interpretation of what a person is feeling or thinking. You can also combine these with the gestures described in the situations demonstrated in the previous chapters.

Conclusion

Thank you again for purchasing this book!

I hope this book was able to help you understand the power of body language and taught you how to apply them to your own benefit. Always keep in mind the importance of knowing what people around you truly feel and how essential it is to control your own body language. It can save you from possible threats, deliver you from trouble, and on a more positive note, help you find your perfect match.

The next step is to practice reading and interpreting non-verbal communication. Never forget to be mindful of your own body signals as well, for other people can sense them. This will take a lot of patience for it is not an easy skill to develop. Nonetheless, the rewards are advantageous.

Thank you and good luck!

www.ingramcontent.com/pod-product-compliance
Lightning Source LLC
Chambersburg PA
CBHW060651290526
45793CB00001B/496